Frankie and Jonny

and Mommy too

Greta S. Marsh

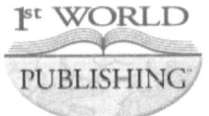
1st WORLD
PUBLISHING

Frankie and Jonny
and Mommy too

Greta S. Marsh

Copyright © Greta S. Marsh 2013

Published by 1stWorld Publishing
P.O. Box 2211, Fairfield, Iowa 52556
tel: 641-209-5000 • fax: 866-440-5234
web: www.1stworldpublishing.com

Third Edition

Originally written in Feb. 1975, second editing in 2003

LCCN: 2013937137
SoftCover ISBN: 978-1-4218-8663-3
HardCover ISBN: 978-1-4218-8664-0

Dedication

To Frankie and Jonny, the Children of South East Asia
and Children Everywhere. Some Day Soon May All Your
Hurting Stop. Some Day Soon May You All Find Peace, Love,
Joy, Happiness and May You All Be Well.

Chapter One
War

It was the month of February 1969
and some of our generals said we were doing just fine.
They said the war in Vietnam would end in no time at all.
Perhaps by next Christmas the enemy would fall.

But this war had been raging for eight bloody years.
You know, wars would not be if people didn't have fears.
Villages had been destroyed and hearts had been stilled.
How awful it is when loved ones are killed.
How awful it is when the innocents are killed.

Fortunately some persons paid no heed
to what those generals said, there were people in need.
Especially children whose parents were dead,
and who had no one to love them and see that they were fed.

Jonny's family was not alone.
There were others who each had room in their home
and adopted these children, some right from the start
because they all had a mountain of love in their hearts.

You see, the love in one's heart was not put there to stay.
If not given to others love tends to decay.
And although many don't know it, they are capable of
caring for others and sharing their love.

Four years earlier mom had been through a divorce.
That didn't make her less capable, of course,
less capable of loving and caring for another child.
But the negative responses she received
might have driven another person wild, real wild.
But not mom. She was determined to persevere and save a child.
But unfortunately there were many who held to that false theory.
They turned her down until she was weary.
She wrote letters, made phone calls, but people said NO!
At times it almost seemed like mom was the foe.

Others said NO because mom was Jewish.
Tell me, thoughtful readers, wasn't that foolish?
To use religion to deny a home to a child
is reason enough to drive you wild.

Fortunately, in Vietnam there was a special nun
who said she'd try to find them a brother and son.
That mother was single she did not care,
and to hold it against her Sister did not think fair.

Sister said it is not true, it is just a fable
that single parents are not able
to raise a daughter or a son
simply because they happen to be one.
Sister was kind. She certainly was not foolish.
She didn't care that Jonny and mom were Jewish.

Chapter Two
Jonny and Mother

Jonny's three sisters were not always at home
and for the very first time he and mom were alone.
His sisters were studying and living at school.
Jonny sure liked mom's attention. He was no fool.

But listen! Mother was talking about boys and girls
who were living in a country called Vietnam,
a country located on the other side of the world.
She was worried because they were starving and dying.
She wanted to help them and stop their crying.

What was it that his mother just said?
A child might come and share his bed?
A child who looked different, whose language was strange?
Had his mother gone crazy? Was her brain deranged?

"Jonny," said mother, "tell me, please do,
just what it is that is troubling you."
That Jonny was troubled mother could tell.
She was so hopeful that her plan would go well.

"I'm not sure that I'll like it," Jonny said, growing bolder.
"Couldn't you please wait until I am older,
older and no longer living at home,
away at college and on my own?

"Now wouldn't that be a great idea?"
Jonny asked, as he wiped away a tear.
Mother replied, "of course we can wait."
She then kissed Jonny's serious face.
She spoke very softly and reassured him
that no one ever would take his place.

"But the heart," she said, "is like a rubber band.
It's like the beach with so much sand
that stretches and stretches for infinite miles
and brings tons of love and tons of smiles.

"Yes, the heart is like a rubber band.
It's a vital organ special and grand
that can stretch and stretch beyond belief
and feel intensely joy and grief."

Now Jonny felt bad because mom looked sad.
But how could he know if this was something he'd like?
It wasn't something simple, like riding a bike.
"Suppose we don't like him and don't want him to stay.
Can we send him back home? Can we send him away?"
"No, a child isn't merchandise," mother said.
She then kissed him good night and he climbed into bed.

A few months passed and Jonny gave some thought
to others in need, as indeed everyone ought.
"Will he speak a strange language and want to sleep on the floor?
Will he want his name tacked up on my door?"

"He'll speak strange at first but learn fast," mother said,
"and after a while he'll like sleeping in a bed.
And if you don't want him to share your room with you,
we'll give him the den and repaint it blue."

As the months passed by and they talked every day,
Jonny grew interested and had a great deal to say.
"He can share my room, play with my toys,
and I'll introduce him to other boys.
How do we get him? What should we do?
How long will it take? What plans should we make?"

Chapter Three
Jonny and Mother
and the Nun

Several weeks passed and mother told Jonny,
"I've written to a nun who runs an orphanage in Govap.
Let's see if we can find it here on this map.
I told her we want to adopt a little boy,
and that doing so would bring us so much joy."

Jonny asked, "How about a boy of ten?"
"I don't know, Jonny. I'll write to Sister again.
But she may think that ten is too old,
too old to adjust, too old to mold."

"Do you think so too?" Jonny asked mother.
A look of concern was on Jonny's face.
You see, he now was anxious for the adoption to take place.
He had matured quite a bit in a short span of time.
Having a new brother made him feel just fine.

His mother was quiet for a moment or two.
She seemed rather anxious and somewhat blue.
"No, I don't think ten is too old," she said with a sigh.
"I certainly would be willing to try."

"I'd prefer ten, but eight or nine will be OK.
I'll teach him to ride, also to slide.
I'll also teach him how to hit a home-run.
It's not easy, but it's something I've sometimes done."

Jonny too wrote to Sister and presented his case.
After reading his letter a smile lit up her face.
Yes, Jonny's letter was read by this busy nun
whose precious little children rarely had any fun.

"I have a special child," she wrote to mother and Jonny.
"He's eight years old. I knew his mommy.
She was killed at Mai Lai. His daddy was a GI.

"I believe you can give him the right kind of care.
Without love and nurturing I don't think he can fare.
Yes, I believe you can provide the right kind of home
for this little child who needs a family of his own."

A touch of gladness and sadness this letter brought.
Jonny now unpacked the mitt he had bought
for his soon-to-be brother, whom he'd teach to play ball,
roller skate and ice skate, shoot for the basket and all.

A few months later another letter arrived.
It was about the child in Govap; not all of them survived.
There was a shortage of food and medicine too.
"I'm afraid, "Sister wrote, "that I have sad news for you.

"The child I wished to place with you suddenly died.
I can tell you no more except that we cried.
He couldn't bear the terrible things he experienced and saw.
Now he's with his mommy and God and at peace forever more."

Mom and Jonny read the letter and cried many tears.
Wars have plagued us throughout the years.
They were angry too because wars don't have to be.
They bring huge benefits to a few, but grief to you and me.

Many months went by and they tried not to think
about the child who had passed; remembering made their
hearts sink.
His eyes looked so sad in the picture they had.
"It's not right," shouted Jonny. He really was mad!
He also was sad. He was very, very sad.

Half a year went by before they heard from the nun.
She wrote that she had another little one.
This little boy was just five years of age.
When Jonny heard that he nearly went into a rage!

"Oh no", Jonny said. "I went down to eight.
Be reasonable, mom. We'll just have to wait
because that's as low as I'll ever go.
Sister will find us another child, I know.

"Mom, what will I do with a five year old brat?
Why, he won't even be able to handle a bat!
I'm seven years older and that's quite a lot.
Mom, what will I do with a five year old tot?"

"I understand how you feel, son; honest I do.
A five year old won't be fun for a big fellow like you.
But this child is in danger; he needs a home.
He needs a family to love him and be his very own.

So let's think of him and not just of us.
C'mon, Jonny, it's not like you to make such a fuss."

"Well, I'll think it over; give me some time."
"That's fair enough Jonny; that's really just fine.
Now finish your homework, dinner is at six.
I've only the salad and spaghetti to fix."

A few days later Jonny told his mother,
"Oh, let him come if Sister can't find us another.
But don't expect me to baby sit
for that kindergarten baby.
And what will I do with this baseball mitt?"

"Your new brother must have an American name.
His Vietnamese name he certainly shall retain.
But Nyugen van Coung will sound strange and funny,
so let's think of a name that sounds cheerful and sunny."

"How about Frankie?" Jonny asked mother.
"Wouldn't that be a good name for my new brother?"
As he spoke, Jonny's eyes became tearful and down cast.
He was thinking about his grandfather who had recently passed.

"Frankie is just perfect," mom said, looking sad.
She and grandpa had been so close.
He'd been such a thoughtful and wonderful dad.

"Your grandpa would like that. You sure are a wonderful lad."
His grandpa had loved him; that Jonny knew.
He'd lived near-by and they'd been so close, those two.

Jonny said nothing for a moment or two.
Mother too was silent and seemed somewhat blue.
"Is it settled? Will it be Frankie?" Jonny inquired.
It was getting late and he was tired.
You see, it had been a very long day:
school, homework and, of course, play!
So he kissed his mom good night and then
fell fast asleep by the count of ten.

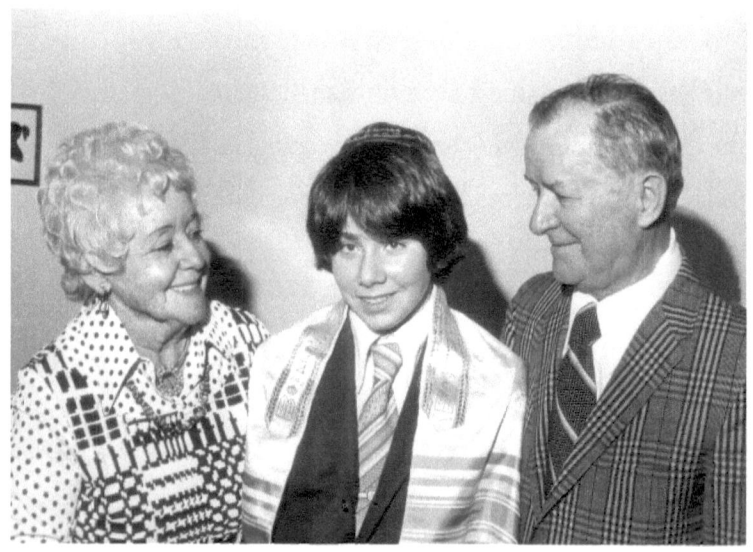

Grandma Margie, Jonny and Papa Frank

Chapter Four
The Govap
Orphanage, Vietnam

And now young readers it is only right
that we move on to
Vietnam, where it was bright day light.
Remember that back in the states where Jonny slept,
it was just the opposite. It was dark, dark night.

Now don't you think that it would be
so very nice if only we
could fly in a space ship across the map
and visit the children who live in Govap?

If only, if only it could be done,
we'd get up real early with only a hint of the sun.
If only, if only it were possible to do,
we'd soar away into the blue,
each one of us in our own spaceship and hark!
We'd arrive in Vietnam where it was not at all dark.

In the Govap Orphanage a few children were still sleeping.
Others were restless and many were weeping.
And although the nuns work hard and do their best,
many children pass away and are laid to rest.
But others were outside having fun
in the early morning of the not-too-hot sun.

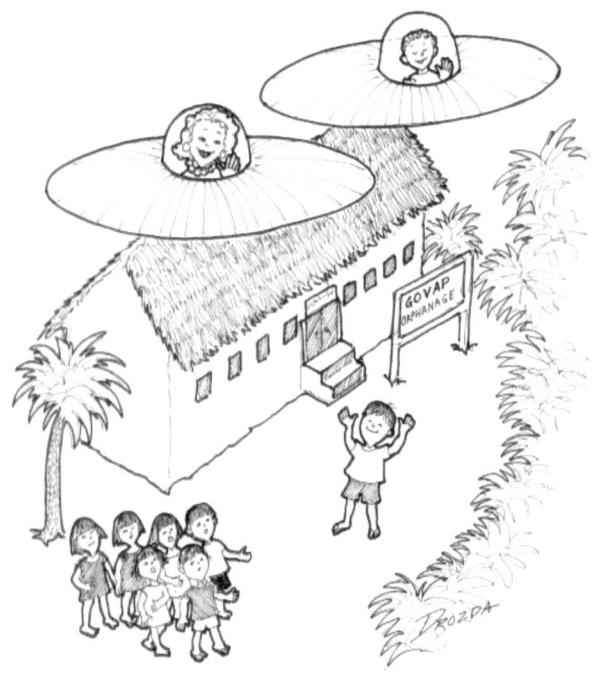

Now close your eyes and perhaps you'll see
Sister at prayer on bended knees
praying for help in caring for
these innocent victims of a brutal and senseless war.

Then she quietly gets up and sits down at a table
and, although quite weary, writes as best as she is able.
You see, it's important to tell mother and Jonny all
she knows about their child before he arrives in the fall.

Sister writes them everything she knows:
their son's name, date of birth and when she's ready to close,
she adds, "This senseless war really has been hell.
This child's parents and entire village fell.
It's a miracle that he even managed to survive.
It's a miracle that he's lived to be five."

Chapter Five
Frankie

Quickly, very quickly, the months passed by
and on that very special day there wasn't a cloud in the sky.
They were up very early and drove to the airport.
In about six months they'd be in the adoption court,
and Frankie would become Jonny's legal brother
and mom would become his legal mother.
Grandma and Aunt Hilda decided to come.
The trip to the airport was both scary and fun.

They were leaving early, mother explained,
to make absolutely certain that they would get
to the airport on time to meet Frankie's jet.
"He'll be frightened seeing so many strange people around,
so let's get there before his plane lands on the ground".

They got into the car and as they drove away
Jonny was talking and you could hear him say,
"Look mom, here's a nice little toy
I bought especially for this little boy."
"This little boy happens to be your new brother,"
Jonny was reminded by his mother.

At the airport they found a place to park.
All four of them felt nervous; this was no lark!
A little boy, whom they had promised to love,
was travelling to them in the sky above.
A precious little boy was on his way.
When they met him, what would they say?

The silver jet landed and they watched as some men
wheeled the plank over to the plane's door and then,
many persons, seeing their loved ones, almost went wild.
Soon a lady appeared holding a child.

He was awfully thin and on his face was a mark.
His eyes were almond shaped, his hair very dark.
Jonny looked hard at his new brother and thought
how sad that this little guy looks so scared.
"I'm going to do my best to make him feel glad.
Glad that now we're a family."

Still looking at his new brother, Jonny hoped
that one day Frankie would adjust and learn how to cope.
Adjust to his new family and new friends,
and to his brand new home and that time would mend
the sadness and hurting that's inside of him.

Mother was thinking he looks so fragile.
"It will take some time but I'm certain that I'll
make him strong and healthy and even fill him with joy.
I just know we'll all love this little boy."
Grandma and Aunt Hilda felt the same.

No other child was on board. He was the only one,
so mom ran over to her brand new son.
Jonny followed close behind.
When mother hugged Frankie, Jonny didn't mind.

Mother held each son gently, one with each arm.
She tried to assure Frankie that he'd come to no harm.
Jonny understood all of this.
He too gave his new brother a kiss.

Jonny felt bad for this little lad.
To travel so far for a family was sad.
During the ride home Frankie tried to act brave.
He sat up straight and accepted the gift Jonny gave
him.

"Gee, I feel sorry for this little guy.
I think I'm really going to like him bye and bye."
He looked kindly at Frankie who responded with a smile.
But behind that smile, tears would linger for a long, long while.

That night Frankie slept in a bed in the same room with his mother.
In that same room in a sleeping bag slept his new brother.
You see, Frankie was not accustomed to a room of his own.
He needed time to get accustomed to his brand, new home.

When a child's thoughts are known only to him,
when he keeps his sadness deep within,
when he's unable to tell us about his fears,
then we must try to comfort him in his tears.

The hurting that's inside some of us is not always seen
by others who are fortunate never to have been
exposed to the terror of shooting and bombing
and the sounds of persons dying and sobbing.

Because only the heart can see things clearly,
we all need someone to love us dearly.
Frankie now had a family: mom, 3 sisters, and a brother,
a loving great aunt and a loving grandmother.
For the present this was fine and he needed no others.

Chapter Six
Frankie and Jonny

That Jonny loved Frankie was easily detected.
He was not the brat Jonny had expected.
Jonny had to admit that Frankie was cute.
He looked especially adorable dressed up in a suit.

They went to a shelter so that Frankie could find
a homeless dog to whom he'd be kind.
When they arrived at the shelter Frankie found
the dog he wanted.
She was a mixed breed with some traces of Dachshund.
Frankie named her Suzie, Suzie Van Cuong.

Her legs were short, her body was long
and her howling sounded like a strange song.
Her ears drooped down and her eyes looked sad.
Was it her eyes that attracted this little lad?

Frankie's bed was built close to the floor
and he and Suzie had fun galore.
They'd hug and slide from the bed to the floor.
They didn't get tired. Yes, they had fun galore.

Jonny and mom had been to the shelter before,
where they had adopted a dog they came to adore.
She was quite precious and had a funny mug.
She had a mashed-in-face. Jonny sometimes called her "Ugh."

Pumkin was funny and certainly never a bore.
She was smart and spunky and boy, did she snore!
Jonny adored Pumkin and her mashed-in nose.
Sometimes he called her Mashed Potatoes!

Jonny looked at the mitt he had bought for the brother
he thought would be around eight or nine.
It was too big for Frankie, so he bought another.
Now he and Frankie would play catch just fine.

Frankie loved the snow that was so white and nice.
Why, he even learned to skate on ice.
He liked to draw all of the things he saw
and when he used up his paper he'd just ask for more.

He smelled a flower and laughed with joy.
So many things delighted this little boy.
He went to the beach and built a sand castle.
Life now was peaceful and no longer a hassle.

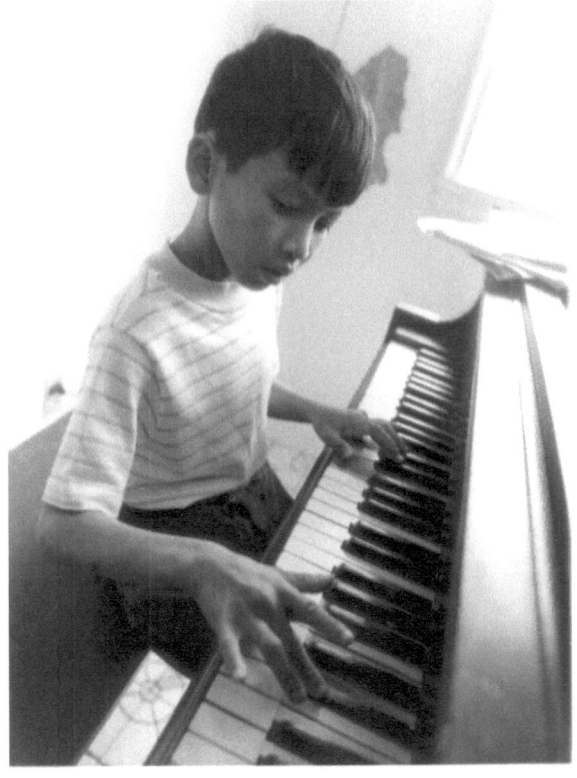

The End

This story has ended and happily one young heart has been mended. There is, however, so much more to say on behalf of children all over the world. May poverty and disease become a thing of their past. May their lives include peace and joy that will last forever and ever and ever.

Epilogue

This story was written a few months before our son and brother arrived from Vietnam in April 1975. He arrived on the Second Baby Air Lift. Several days earlier the First Baby Air Lift had crashed and all on board perished. He had already been baptized David in an orphanage, so we named him David Frank, after the grandfather he never knew. Had Poppa Frank lived, he would have loved David Frank as dearly as his grandmother Margaret and great Aunt Hilda did and as dearly as his mother, brother and three sisters do. "Frankie and Jonny" is basically factual. Fictionalized portions are the result of an informed imagination.

Of the 3.2 million Americans who served in the Vietnam War, 58,229 perished. The men and women who did survive, so many of whom are physically and spiritually broken, were rebuffed by the American people and the United States government. Their physical , emotional and financial needs have been severely neglected and they number heavily among the poor and homeless, as do veterans of past and present wars and so-called "operations."

The construction of the Vietnam Veterans' Memorial in Washington, DC in 1982 finally pays tribute to the men and women who perished in that war (it never was officially declared a war). But so much more needs to be done for the survivors and their families. The same is true for the survivors of other wars or "operations" of both the past and present - Iraq and Afghanistan - and their families. Too few Americans are aware of their horrific pain, misery and suffering.

Americans everywhere should contact their representatives and senators in Washington, D.C. and urge them not to decrease veterans' benefits. Not only should they not be decreased; indeed, their benefits should be increased. Substantially! This is the least we can do for those who served and continue to serve their country in times of war and other so-called "operations."

Whether we agreed/agree with or opposed/oppose any or all of these wars or "operations" is not the issue. All of us, especially the U.S. government, owe these men and women more than I am able to express. Their care and well-being are the responsibility of all of us. Anything less is disgraceful, shameful and unconscionable.

Greta Marsh
Long Beach, N.Y.
Lanesboro, MA
Easthampton, MA
Feb. 1975, April 2003
and April 2012

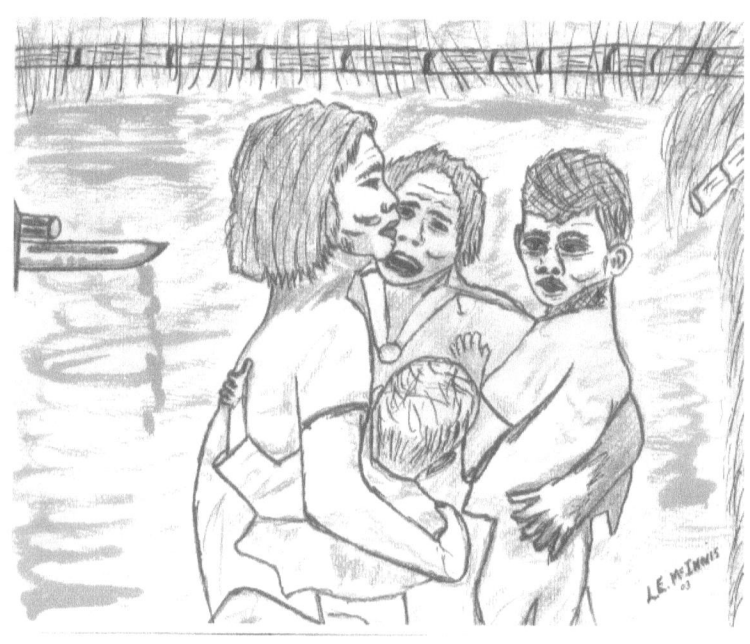

ANGUISH
L. E. McInnis
Vietnam veteran

Some Sad and Mad Facts about Wars

Please note that my references to American military personnel include U.S. Air Force, Army, Marines, Navy and Paratroopers. Source of Information: The Nation, Fall 2012, the newspaper published by Vietnam Veterans Against the War. (vvaw@vvaw.org).

My Lai

In March 1968, in the village of My Lai in Vietnam, American military lost all sense of reason and sanity and shot and brutally murdered unarmed civilians - men, women, children and babies. Methods used included assaults, rapes, torture, sodomy and maimings. These were committed individually and in groups. The platoon leader, Lt. William Calley, was the instigator and a participant. He was court martialed for the premeditated murder of 22 or more Vietnamese civilians, was convicted and sentenced to life in prison. The other American military personnel either were acquitted or the charges were dropped.

Three years later Calley was granted a pardon by President Nixon. (Vietnam Savagery by David Lavery, P. 30, The Veteran).

Suicide

More American military personnel in Iraq and Afghanistan died and continue to die by suicide than by enemy fire. Veterans of these two wars who are between the ages of 20 and 24 are two to four times more likely to to take their own lives than are 20 to 24 year old civilians. In addition, among active military personnel, about eighteen commit suicide each month; the rate among veterans is about eighteen per day. (Army Suicides, by John Ketwig, p.26, The Veteran). More than 12,000 Afghan civilians have been killed since 2006 and more than 185,000 were displaced in 2011, a 45% increase since 2010. (articles by Jon Mitchell, pp. 20 and 22, and Sara Lazare, p. 28 The Veteran).

Rape and Sexual Harassment

About 30% of women in the military have reported being the victims of rape or attempted rape, while about 75% report being sexually harassed. (Truth in Recruiting: Questions, by Michael Orange, p. 19, The Veteran).

Physical Injuries and Damages Suffered from Agent Orange, Dioxins and Napalm During the war in Vietnam

American and Vietnamese military personnel and Vietnamese civilians suffered severely from enemy fire: blindness, paralysis, brain damage and blown off limbs or limbs that had to be surgically removed. In addition, they suffer and continue to suffer from the deadly affects of Agent Orange, Dioxins and Napalm, which were routinely, heavily and indiscriminately used through out that ravaged country. Diseases include but are not limited to cancers, heart disease and diabetes, not just in American and Vietnamese veterans and Vietnamese civilians, but also in their children and grandchildren. In addition, some of the latter have been and continue to be born minus limbs or fingers and toes. Like their veteran parents and grandparents, their lifespans are a good deal shortened. The purpose of the lethal spraying was to destroy all vegetation (forests, jungles, trees and family land) so that Vietnamese military and civilians would be unable to find cover from enemy fire. (The Peace Boat, pp.25 and 26, The Veteran).

Recently, a national coordinator of Vietnam Veterans Against the War visited Vietnam, where she met with and saw second and third generation babies and children. Some were born with enlarged heads, bulging eyes, bodies filled with tremors and bodies that were twisted or rigid. Some were unable to speak. These tragedies were caused by American aircraft that sprayed the above-mentioned lethal herbicides. (Revisiting Vietnam, by Susan Schmall, pp.1 and 21, and US Children of Vietnam Vets Bring Message of Solidarity to Okinawa, by Jon Mitchell, pp. 20 and 22, The Veteran). MS. Schmall advises that a 2011 bill (HR 2634), which would have provided relief for these victims, failed to pass in Congress.

On a more personal level, there is the story about a young woman whose American soldier father was exposed to Agent Orange in Vietnam. He underwent five heart bypasses at age 38, developed diabetes at 40 and died from a massive heart attack at age 50. This courageous lady, who is 39, was born 2 months premature, minus her right leg below the knee, and minus several fingers and the big toe on her left foot. (Jon Mitchell, pp. 20 and 22, The Veteran).

The Vietnam War caused 6 million casualties in S.E. Asia, among them 4.7 million civilians. The number reported for American military dead or missing in this article is 60,209. (Truth in Recruiting: Questions, by Michael Orange, P.19, The Veteran). I previously reported 58,229 American deaths, which would leave about 1,980 Americans missing.

Percent of Civilian Casualties in Wars

WW 1   15%

WW 2   65%

Korea   70%

Vietnam   85%

Iraq   93% : between 800,000 - 1.2 million civilian deaths.

(Truth in Recruiting: Questions, by Michael Orange, p. 19, The Veteran).

American Casualties in Iraq: 4,384 reported dead or missing; 31, 716 reported wounded. (please note that wounded comes in many degrees: functional and non functional and brain and/ or physically wounded). About 30% of veterans who fought in Vietnam, Iraq and Afghanistan (and who continue to fight in Afghanistan) develop long term, debilitating PTSD. (Ibid)

Total Number of U.S. Military Interventions in Other Countries: 147; Total Number since WW 2: 44 (Ibid).

Michael Orange also reports that Julian Bond was expelled from the Georgia House of Representatives for opposing the war in Vietnam. Former Representative Bond then wrote a comic called "Vietnam," which was written and published in 1967. It can be read on line. (Ibid).

Many Thanks to Vietnam Veterans Against the War for all they do to teach about the horrors of Wars, Promote Peace, and constantly "be there" for needy veterans and their families. (vvaw@vvaw.org). Similar helping organizations include Iraq Veterans Against the War (ivaw.org) that was organized with the help and financial support of VVAW, Veterans for Peace (veteransforpeace.org) and The Civilian-Soldiers Alliance (civsol.org). To obtain information about Afghanistan veterans and civilians contact ivaw.org/avaw.

Another commendable organization is Veterans of the Vietnam War and the Veterans' Coalition. It was founded by Mike Milne and became a chartered organization in 1980 under the original name of Veterans of the Vietnam War. Mike Milne served in Vietnam from 1962 to 1969. Although he suffered severely from the affects of Agent Orange and was certified as 100% disabled, he worked tirelessly on behalf of other Vietnam veterans who likewise suffered. In 1998 the Beacon House Project was founded in response to the huge numbers of Vietnam veterans who were living on the streets. Its mission was to provide safe and transitional housing for them until they could reintegrate into civilian life. They were suffering mentally and physically.

In September 2004 the name was enlarged in order to include veterans of all wars. It is estimated that 1/3 of homeless persons in the United States are war veterans. Although ill, Mr. Milne was a POW-MIA activist and served as vice chairman of the National Vietnam and Gulf War Coalition until 2003, when he resigned because of failing health. This caring man passed away in 2007 from complications of Agent Orange. Appropriately, the organization's motto is "People Who Care." Mr. Milne was 63. It should be noted that Agent Orange destroyed lives not just in Vietnam, but also in Laos and Cambodia.

The present leader of this organization (National Commander) is Peter Forbes, an Australian. He was drafted in Australia, served in the 3rd Australian regiment and was sent to Vietnam where he served as a combat medic in 1970 and 1971. Several other countries sent military personnel to Vietnam, among them Korea, New Zealand and Burma. Veterans of the Vietnam War and the Veterans' Coalition now is an international organization.

Vietnam veterans comprise the largest segment of homeless veterans - 58%; 3% are World War 2 veterans; 14% are Korean War veterans and 25% are from the post Vietnam War era - the Gulf, Iraq and Afghanistan wars. Mr. Forbes and his dedicated staff and volunteers share Mike Milne's passion for helping veterans of all wars. Beacon Houses have thrived under his leadership and at present twenty two are located in New York, one in South Dakota, one in Pennsylvania and more are being planned in other states. The Beacon House Project also operates food pantries for needy veterans and their families, assists incarcerated veterans and their families, provides needed casework assistance for veterans and their families and sends Support Packages to military personnel serving overseas and their families.

There are other worthy organizations that assist needy veterans and their families who deserve our thanks and cooperation.

More Mad and Sad Facts About Wars: Laos and Cambodia

The Vietnam War extended into both Laos and Cambodia as did lethal herbicides such as Agent Orange. Regarding Laos, it has been reported that spraying took place on approximately 209 days between 1965 and 1970 and a total of at least 537,495 gallons were sprayed. It is believed that the areas sprayed most frequently were located along the Ho Chi Minh Trail because it extends along the borders of Laos, Vietnam and Cambodia and was routinely used by the Viet Cong. The bombing and use of herbicides in Laos was kept secret until 1982, when it was made public in response to the Freedom of Information Act. It is not certain if the spraying was done by hand or by helicopters.

Cambodia was not as systematically sprayed as was Laos but the lethal herbicide mist drifted from Vietnam into Cambodia. One direct spraying, however, is recorded to have occurred between April 18 and May 2, 1969, causing severe and lethal damage to human and foliage life. In 1969 the Cambodian government filed claims against the U.S. government for $12.2 million in damages. Henry Kissinger, National Security Advisor to Nixon, strongly opposed this claim and succeeded in delaying payment until fiscal year 1972. In April 1970, Nixon ordered U.S. troops to attack Cambodia because some believed a Communist base was located there. Nixon denied that it was an extension of the Vietnam War and described it as an effort to get North Vietnam forces out of Cambodia.

It has been suggested that since Vietnam, Laos and Cambodia comprise the peninsula of Indochina, it would be more accurate to call the war the Indochina War.

Update

After South Vietnam fell in 1975 Greta and Jonny never heard again from Sister Marie Angela. They were unable to contact her and do not know what became of her and the children in the Govap orphanage. They do not know what became of the child who was to be their son and brother. David Frank came into their lives via a Denver, Colorado - based organization in April 1975.

Hope

Governments treat wars as if they were a game. Games they are not. They are a deadly and vicious shame. If only some day they called a war and nobody would come, then good people everywhere will have won and what a wonderful world this would be. Oh, what a wonderful world this would be!

About the Author

In late 1991, after retiring from the Nassau County Probation Department in New York, the author moved to Lanesboro, MA and started rescuing horses (and 2 calves). At about the same time, motivated by the horrible experience of Shayna, her first adopted Greyhound, Greta started the movement to end dog racing in MA. It was a 17 year struggle that finally was won in November 2008.

At present the author resides in Easthampton, MA with three 4 legged friends, Greyhounds, and a 2 legged friend. She is working hard on behalf of S 541 and HR 1094, 2 bills that are awaiting action in Congress. If they become law, horses will be protected from tortuous slaughter and people will be protected from horse flesh that is filled with medications and chemicals that are toxic to humans.

OTHER BOOKS BY THE AUTHOR: The Story of MY Life, by Shayna as told to Greta.

www.ingramcontent.com/pod-product-compliance
Lightning Source LLC
Chambersburg PA
CBHW021930170526
45157CB00005B/2258